Bad Code Smells

Tips and Tricks to Refactor Effectively

Table of Contents

Chapter 1. Introduction

Diving into the realm of programming code is an adventure, wrapped in layers of logical thinking, problem-solving, and continuous learning. One such intriguing journey is our understanding and mitigation of "Bad Code Smells." Here's an enriching Special Report, intended to empower programmers, developers, software architects, and everyone else with an interest in code excellence. This report demystifies a highly technical subject with an easy-to-understand, down-to-earth approach. It highlights effective tips and tricks to refactor these so-called bad code smells – those hints or symptoms in the code that possibly indicate deeper issues. It does so with a keen focus on practical, hands-on solutions that can be readily applied to your everyday coding routines. The objective is to augment programmer productivity and code efficiency, with a firm belief that the process of refactoring need not be a daunting task. Dive in, embark on this insightful journey into code refactoring, and elevate your coding skills.

Chapter 2. Understanding Bad Code Smells: An Introduction

When you're engrossed in writing code, with an ambitious goal in mind and a deadline looming ahead, it's easy to forget about the bigger picture. But often the most critical aspect of any code lies within its design, and more specifically, how easily it can be read, understood, and modified by yourself and your fellow programmers in the future. Herein lies our introduction to a concept known as 'Bad Code Smells.'

2.1. What are 'Bad Code Smells?'

"Bad Code Smells" is a term coined by Kent Beck, a pioneer in the field of software engineering, in the seminal work 'Refactoring: Improving the Design of Existing Code' he co-authored with Martin Fowler. Essentially, a code smell is a surface-level problem—an issue that you may notice first before delving deeper into the code—that clues you into deeper, more inherent issues found within your code.

To think of it in a more literal sense, if you noticed a curious odor in your home, you'd likely investigate further to find its source. Perhaps it's a piece of rotting food, a nest of bugs, or even a dangerous gas leak. You won't know until you investigate that smell. Similarly, a bad code smell might hint at something much deeper—perhaps an entrenched design issue that could pose serious, systemic issues if not treated properly.

2.2. Types of Bad Code Smells

There are many types of bad code smells. Each of these reflects different issues within your code—small indicators of larger problems that could potentially become major issues if not treated appropriately. Here are some of the more common bad smells you might come across:

1. Long Method: A method that has grown too large is difficult to understand and debug. It's also challenging to recall what exactly such code does, especially when returning to it after a significant lapse of time. Remedying this often involves 'Extract Method' refactoring, where you break down the method into smaller, more easily managed sections.

2. Large Class: Similar to the Long Method smell, a class that has become too large can be complex to maintain, understand, and troubleshoot. Resolving this issue often involves applying 'Extract Class' refactoring to create more coherent, manageable classes.

3. Data Clumps: These are groups of data that always seem to be hanging around together. If you always see the same data travelling together around different parts of your code, that could signal a missed opportunity to bundle this data into a class. Mitigating this involves 'Extract Class' or 'Introduce Parameter Object' refactoring.

4. Primitive Obsession: This smell manifests when primitive data types are overly used to represent domain ideas. For instance, using an integer or string to represent a date instead of a Date object. Overcoming this issue involves 'Replace Data Value with Object' or 'Replace Type Code with Class' refactoring.

5. Long Parameter List: Functions or methods sporting long input parameter lists are difficult to understand and hence maintain. We can use 'Replace Parameter with Method' or 'Introduce Parameter Object' refactoring to clear up this issue.

The list above is by no means exhaustive, but shines a light on the primary culprits often found in code that hasn't been given the required attention over time.

2.3. The Costs of Ignoring Code Smells

While bad code smells in themselves are not bugs or errors in the code's functionality, they do point out design inefficiencies. Untreated, this could lead to several potential issues:

- Difficulty in maintaining the code

- An increased likelihood of bugs being introduced

- Trouble in understanding code's purpose

Hence, ignoring these warning signs might result in poor software performance, confusing code structures, and ultimately an overall decrease in the team's productivity.

2.4. How to Mitigate Bad Code Smells

If you identify a code smell, several techniques, collectively known as Refactoring, can be effectively implemented for its mitigation. The term 'refactoring' refers to changes that programmers make to their code to fight off these smells without altering its external behavior.

Refactoring demands a clean, disciplined approach to altering your code. One critical point to remember here is that refactoring is not a one-time procedure; it's instead a continuous process, a part of the daily coding routine.

The existence of 'Bad Code Smells' doesn't mean that something is wrong or that the person who wrote the code is a poor developer. These are merely hints or indicators of possible improvements one can make to enhance the code's maintainability, readability, and longevity. After all, the better the state of the code, the easier it will be for you and your peers to understand and edit in the future.

By acknowledging 'Bad Code Smells', you are taking steps towards improved code quality and more effective and efficient project management. Armed with the knowledge of these smells and the mechanisms to refactor them, your journey towards pristine, well-maintained code can truly begin. The report's upcoming chapters shall delve deeper into each code smell type and provide practical, approachable guideposts to refactor them effectively.

Chapter 3. Symptoms of Bad Code Smells

When dealing with code, it's often easier to identify that there's a problem rather than pinpointing the specific issue. Bad code smells, or poor design choices, act as red flags that signify deeper problems down the line. Recognizing these symptoms is the first step towards effective refactoring and overall better code health.

3.1. What Constitutes a "Code Smell"?

To get better at identifying code smells, we must first understand what they are. Essentially, a code smell is a characteristic in the source code that signals a deeper problem. It's not a bug—meaning it won't produce erroneous output or results—but it does pose challenges in terms of code maintainability, readability, and extensibility.

The concept of a "code smell" is subjective to a certain degree and relies on the perception of the developer. However, some signs are universal and are generally agreed upon as indicators of suboptimal design. They are not necessarily errors but often highlight the areas needing design improvements.

3.2. Common Symptoms of Code Smells

Let's now delve into the specifics and explore some of the most common symptoms indicative of bad code smells.

1. **Long Methods:** Longer methods are harder to maintain,

understand, and debug. If a method is performing too many operations, then it might be breaking the Single Responsibility Principle (SRP). A good rule of thumb is if it's challenging to describe what the method does without using the word "and," the method probably has too many responsibilities.

2. **Large Class:** A large class, like a long method, tends to break SRP and often becomes a challenge to maintain. These classes often accumulate many responsibilities with subsequent software evolutions and become a hotspot for bugs.

3. **Duplicated Code:** One of the earliest principles we learn as programmers is DRY—Don't Repeat Yourself. Duplicate code should be refactored into a single method and then called multiple times. Duplication indicates poor abstraction and leads to higher maintenance costs as changes necessitate modifications in multiple places.

4. **God Object:** A God object refers to an object that knows too much or does too much, hence violating the principles of Encapsulation and Abstraction. Such an object becomes a labyrinth, making it almost impossible to isolate dependencies and repercussions of changes made to them.

5. **Feature Envy:** A method that seems more interested in a class other than the one it actually is in. It accesses the data of other classes more than its own data. This might indicate that the method is misplaced, and it belongs to a different class.

6. **Data Clumps:** When you see the same few data items grouped together in lots of places, it could point towards a missing class. If you always see the same data hanging around together, maybe it belongs together.

7. **Refused Bequest:** This happens when a subclass uses only a portion of the methods and properties of its superclass. If a subclass doesn't use what it inherits, it's a sign that inheritance isn't the right mechanism in this context.

8. **Inappropriate Naming:** Names should clearly articulate what

variable, classes, or methods they represent. Inappropriately named entities often cause unnecessary confusion and make the code hard to understand.

9. **Incomplete or incorrect implementation of libraries or frameworks:** If a library or framework is used in an unconventional manner or incorrectly, they become a stumbling block for everyone who tries to understand the code.

3.3. Mitigating Symptoms of Code Smells

Once we've identified the symptoms, it's crucial to address these issues with effective refactoring strategies. Refactoring becomes an essential part of code quality and maintainability, leading to efficient debugging and regression testing.

Curbing these smells involves a structured approach wherein each of the symptoms is addressed individually, understanding their root cause and rectifying them by employing well-established programming principles, patterns, and best practices such as DRY, KISS (Keep It Simple, Stupid), YAGNI (You Aren't Going to Need It), and SOLID principles.

Key points to remember while refactoring:

1. Always ensure to have a reliable and comprehensive set of automated tests before refactoring, to check that behavior hasn't changed after modifications.

2. It's often better to do small, incremental refactorings than large, drastic changes, which could introduce new bugs.

3. Continuous refactoring should be part of the development process, rather than being relegated to a separate phase.

4. The aim is to deliver customer value. Hence, refactoring should

increase the value of the software to the customer, either by improving understanding, making future changes easier, speeding up the software, reducing memory footprint, or eliminating potential future errors.

3.4. Conclusion

Bad code smells are not necessarily incorrect code but indicate deeper issues that could potentially deteriorate the codebase's maintainability and legibility. By learning to identify these signs, you stand to increase longevity and scalability of your code, reduce debugging and maintenance time, and, most importantly, elevate your journey as a developer.

Chapter 4. Anatomy of Refactoring: A Deeper Insight

Programming's delights emanate not only from the creation of novel solutions but also from the unbundling, understanding, and improving of existing ones—refactoring. While refactoring in its most basic sense implies the alteration of an application's source code—altered to improve readability, simplicity, and maintainability without changing its external behavior—there's much more to it.

In an endeavor to unearth the dynamics of refactoring, let's delve into its anatomy, straddling through its intricacies, implications, and applications.

4.1. Understanding Refactoring

Refactoring is a disciplined technique for restructuring an existing body of code, altering its internal structure without altering its external behavior. Its primary motive is to fight software deterioration. By transforming a chaotic mass of code into a healthily structured, easily comprehensible entity, refactoring can indeed extend the life of software, easing future enhancements.

Although seemingly effortless, refactoring necessitates impeccable accuracy to prevent the destruction of the code's essence. The process can be compared to a flawless surgery, leaving no trace of its execution but instead enhancing the overall system health.

4.2. Objectives of Refactoring

Multiple objectives drive the need for refactoring in our coding rituals:

1. Improving the Design of Software: Refactoring makes improvements in software design, fighting degradation as we continuously update it with new features.

2. Making Software Easier to Understand: Refactoring clarifies the mystifying segments of code, making it readily understandable to others and ourselves in the future.

3. Helping Find Bugs: By simplifying code and enhancing its readability, refactoring enables more straightforward detection and correction of bugs.

4. Facilitating Programming Speed: Over time, refactoring accelerates software development as the code becomes easier to comprehend and manipulate.

4.3. Refactoring Techniques

Several refactoring techniques provide diverse ways to clean and improve the structure of your code. These include:

1. Extract Method: Here, we take a code fragment that can be grouped, move it into a separate new method, and replace the old code with a call to the method.

2. Inline Method: This technique looks at a method whose content can fit into its call, hence, it replaces calls to the method with the method's content and deletes the method itself.

3. Hide Delegate: In this method, a client gets data and calls a method from an object in another class. Instead of communicating directly with this object, the class creates a new method that redirects the caller to that object.

4. Extract Variable: If an expression in your program is getting hard to understand, put the result of such an expression in a new local variable which self-describes the purpose of expression.

5. Inline Temp: Here, one moves the expression to the body of the

method, replacing all references to temp.

These are just a few techniques. Multiple strategies suit complex scenarios, each harking back to the principle of making the code cleaner and more efficient without altering its behavior.

4.4. The Art of Spotting Code Smells

Before we start refactoring, we must comprehend the 'why.' It's crucial to recognize the telltale signs- the 'code smells' that signify the need for refactoring. Code smells refer to any characteristic in the source code that possibly indicates a deeper problem.

Recognizing 'code smells' is the first step in the refactoring journey. Some common code smells include complicated code that's hard to understand or modify, duplicate code, large classes or methods, high complexity, and many others. The intent should be to ensure that the code remains 'DRY' – Don't Repeat Yourself, and 'KISS'- Keep It Simple and Straightforward.

4.5. Tools for Refactoring

Equally as important as understanding 'why' and 'how' of refactoring, one must also equip oneself with the right tools. Various refactoring tools can make the process easier and more effective. For instance, IDEs (Integrated Development Environments) like IntelliJ IDEA, Eclipse, and NetBeans offer built-in refactoring tools that help to automate and streamline the refactoring process.

Apart from IDEs, many standalone tools can assist, like Resharper, CodeRush, and JRefactory. These tools usually provide features such as code analysis, reporting, and even automated refactoring operations. They are dedicated to making your code cleaner, simpler, and easier to understand.

4.6. Pitfalls and Precautions

However indispensable, refactoring also has its pitfalls. If applied thoughtlessly, refactoring can sometimes lead to more harm than benefit. Keeping the following in mind can help prevent mishaps:

1. Test Coverage: Before embarking on refactoring, ensure you have a robust set of tests for your code. It provides a safety net that helps you uncover any unintended changes in behavior.

2. Incremental Changes: To keep refactoring under control, one should proceed with small, incremental changes rather than dramatic overhauls. Remember, refactoring is like a financial investment, with small, regular deposits being safer and more effective than one-time, large deposit.

3. Understanding Trade-offs: Refactoring is not always the solution to code smells. At times, other factors such as tight deadlines or very old, brittle code may necessitate postponing refactoring. Understanding these trade-offs is crucial.

In conclusion, refactoring is a sophisticated dance that requires precision, understanding, and most importantly, finesse. By understanding its intricate process, spotting the 'code smells', and wielding the right set of tools, we can master this art, thereby enhancing our code's efficiency, readability, and maintainability. With diligence and practice, refactoring can indeed become an integral part of our everyday coding rituals.

Chapter 5. Picking up the Scent: Identifying Bad Code Smells

Understanding how to identify bad code smells is the first crucial step in the refactoring process, but what do we actually mean when we say 'bad code smells?' They're essentially hints or signs that the code in question has a deeper issue that's not entirely apparent at first glance. The code might work, but there could be hidden bugs, the design might not be optimal, or the code could be harder to maintain than it needs to be. Let's dive a little deeper to understand and identify these smells.

5.1. Types of Code Smells

There are various types of code smells; these fall into several categories based on their characteristics.

1. **Bloaters:** Bloated code is filled with classes or methods that have grown to such monstrous sizes that they're hard to work with. Under Bloaters, we look into Long Method, Large Class, Primitive Obsession, Long Parameter List, and Data Clumps.

2. **Object-Orientation Abusers:** This category comprises smells related to incorrect use of object-oriented principles. It includes Switch Statements, Temporary Field, Refused Bequest, and Alternative Classes with Different Interfaces.

3. **Change Preventers:** Code smells in this category make it harder to make changes to the code. They include Divergent Change, Shotgun Surgery, and Parallel Inheritance Hierarchies.

4. **Dispensables:** These are elements of the code that make understanding it harder, and could be removed without reducing

the code's functionality such as Duplicate Code, Lazy Class, Data Class, Dead Code, and Speculative Generality.

5. **Couplers:** These smells introduce unnecessary coupling between classes that should be uncoupled, such as Inappropriate Intimacy, Message Chains, Middle Man, Divergent Change, and Feature Envy.

Let's discuss each category and a few of its contributing smells in more detail.

5.2. Bloaters

Bloaters are parts of code that have become so overwhelmed by their own growth that they have become burdensome, hard to work with, or virtually unmanageable.

Long Method

The most common smell is the long method, characterized by a method that has become a sprawling, convoluted monster. A well-designed method should ideally perform a single operation and be easily understandable. A quick tip would be limiting the length of methods, although that is by no means a hard and fast rule.

```
def long_method(a, b, c, d, e)
  // A segment of complex code
end
```

A key to refactoring this smell is breaking up the method into smaller sub-methods, each with their explicit purpose.

Large Class

A class that's trying to do too much can become a bloated beast that's hard to maintain. How do you know it's too large? Signs might include a high number of instance variables or methods that only use a part of the class's properties. Large classes are usually harder to debug and understand.

```
class LargeClass
  // A large number of attributes and methods
end
```

Refactoring often involves splitting the large class into smaller, more focused classes.

5.3. Object-Orientation Abusers

These smells occur when the principles of object-oriented programming are not applied properly, leading to convoluted and hard-to-maintain code.

Temporary Field

Temporary fields get their values (and thus become useful) only under certain circumstances. Outside of these circumstances, they are empty.

```
class TemporaryField
  int temp = 0;

  void someMethod() {
    temp = 30;
    // use temp
  }
end
```

Refactoring often involves rethinking the class design, potentially splitting the class, or potentially getting rid of the temporary field entirely and passing its data in a different way.

Switch Statements

This code smell occurs when a switch statement's complexity is widespread and duplicated in the system. Repeated switch statements can become a code maintenance nightmare because adding a new condition implies updating all the switch statements' code in the system.

Here's an example that hints at a switch statement smell:

```
switch (type) {
  case TYPE1:
    // behavior for type 1
    break;
  case TYPE2:
    // behavior for type 2
    break;
  // more cases
}
```

Refactoring might involve applying polymorphism to solve this problem, where each operation is placed within its own method in different classes corresponding to different types.

5.4. Recognize The Smell

Detecting a smell isn't always easy and there isn't a hard and fast rule. However, there are indicators that when noted, should prompt a reaction:

- A routine is hard to understand

- The need to spend time looking at piece of code from different parts often

- The need to introduce comments indicating a problem

There's no one-size-fits-all solution to every code smell. The key point is that once we recognize a code smell, we can then look to our refactoring toolbox for strategies to improve the code. The next chapters will elaborate more on those refactoring strategies.

Remember, code smells don't always signify real problems. Sometimes, they are simply quirks in the developer's style or the constraints of the project. So while it's essential to recognize these smells and understand what they often mean, it's just as important not to become a "code smell extremist," rushing to refactor every whiff of a problem. Balance and understanding are key.

Chapter 6. Duplications in Code: The Copy-Paste Syndrome

6.1. Understanding Code Duplication

Code duplication, fondly referred to as the "Copy-Paste Syndrome," is one of the most common occurrences of bad code smells in software development. It unfolds when blocks of code are replicated across different parts of the codebase, leading to redundancies. This might seem like an easy solution when faced with pressing deadlines, but these cut corners can lead to convoluted code and maintenance issues in the future.

6.2. Origin and Implications

Code duplication can stem from various reasons. Often, when developers find a code chunk performing a specific function, they tend to reproduce it wherever the similar functionality is needed without understanding the long-term implications of this action. At first, this 'copy-paste-edit' routine may seem like a time-saving maneuver. However, as the codebase grows and evolves, the detrimental effects of this practice surface.

When an alteration needs to be made, one might have to dig through the entire codebase to adjust each duplicated block accordingly. This amplifies the risk of errors and inconsistencies, while drastically reducing the ease of maintaining and testing the codebase. Further, if a bug is discovered in a duplicated code section, it might be present in all the copies, necessitating a wider search and comprehensive debugging.

Additionally, code duplication is contrary to one of the most basic principles of software development: Don't Repeat Yourself (DRY), leading to a more difficult-to-modify codebase.

6.3. Identifying Code Duplication

There are varied forms of code duplication. They might range from a few lines of replicated code to similar methods, classes, or even entire modules and packages. Some instances are clearly visible and detectable, while others, especially those involving changes over time or across developers, can be more elusive.

To aid in the identification of code duplication, we can enlist several tools. The category of software known as 'duplicate code detection tools' can prove incredibly useful here. They can detect exact and near-miss copies in your codebase, presenting a comprehensive overview of the extent to which code duplication has infested your application. Some widely-accepted tools include Simian, PMD's Copy/Paste Detector (CPD), and SonarQube.

It is essential to understand that the tools are mere facilitators; recognizing and preventing code duplication requires a conscious effort and disciplinary integrity from the development team.

6.4. Treatment of Code Duplication

Once code duplication is identified, the next step would be to mitigate it. Refactoring is an effective method in this regard, where the aim is to alter the internal structure of the code to make it efficient, without affecting external behavior.

Refactoring of duplicated code elements generally involves the following strategies:

1. Abstract common code into separate methods or functions - If the replicated block is a series of statements, consider creating a method that embodies these statements. This way, any requisite modifications in the future will only be made in one place.

2. Encapsulate common code into separate classes (if not already an object) - Encapsulating repetitive code into a class promotes encapsulation and abstraction principles in Object-Oriented Programming (OOP).

3. Use polymorphism - For duplicate code within derived classes, using polymorphism, through method overriding, helps in discarding the need for duplicate code.

4. Use design patterns - Design patterns, like Template Method or Strategy, provide higher-level pathways to eliminate code repetition.

It is also important to consider comprehensibility alongside removing duplication. A straightforward repetitive code could be better than a convoluted DRY solution.

6.5. Code Duplication Prevention

While eliminating existing duplications is crucial, it's equally important to prevent future occurrences. This can be achieved by:

1. Encouraging developers to grasp the full scope of the codebase - This will enable them to identify and reuse existing functions or methods instead of creating new, repetitive ones.

2. Organizing regular code reviews - A fresh pair of eyes may catch duplications that the original programmers could not.

3. Incorporating duplicate detection tools into your development process - Regular scans can help identify duplications early on and reduce the ripple effects.

By recognizing and countering the implications of code duplication, we can drastically improve the quality of our codebase, making it more manageable and comprehensive. Remember that an ounce of prevention is worth a pound of cure, and this holds especially true in case of code duplication. This intricate dance between prevention, identification, and refactoring will help you build not just better code, but also become a more mindful programmer.

Chapter 7. Coupled Code and Distant Changes: Overcoming Over-Dependency

Code coupling is an inevitable part of software development. In well-designed software, components depend on each other to a limit that promotes functionality while maintaining modularity. The problem arises when this interaction becomes excessive, leading to what we refer to as 'over-dependency.' Over-dependency gives rise to issues like difficulty in maintenance, lack of flexibility, and an increase in the chance of bugs popping up in the system.

7.1. Understanding Coupled Code

The first step in tackling this issue head-on is to understand what we mean by coupled code. In layman's terms, coupled code is when one part of the program heavily relies on another part to function. Class A depends so much on Class B that even the slightest changes in Class B may lead to Class A's failure. Such a situation creates a fragile ecosystem vulnerable to various sorts of bugs and issues.

7.2. Identifying Coupled Code

To identify what pieces of your program are excessively interlinked, you should be vigilant of symptoms like:

- Changes in one class or module often force adjustments in another.

- Duplication of code.

- One class contains the data and functions of another class.

- Classes are overly large.

If any of these symptoms are present in your application, then it's high time you showed the red flag and brought in the refactor cavalry.

7.3. Techniques to Tackle Coupled Code

Once the issue at hand is understood and identified, it's time to counteract it. This can be achieved by following certain design principles and applying refactoring techniques which promote low coupling and high cohesion.

1. *Use Abstraction:* Introducing interfaces and abstract classes can reduce the dependency between different modules. You can define what a class does through an interface or an abstract class, and let the class implement the details.

2. *Dependency Injection:* This technique involves supplying dependencies of one object from another object.

3. *Single Responsibility Principle:* This principle dictates that a class or module should have one, and only one, reason to change. By doing so, it reduces coupling and makes the code easier to understand and maintain.

4. *Refactoring:* Techniques such as 'Extract Method,' 'Extract Class,' 'Move Method,' 'Move Field,' and 'Rename Method' can be utilized.

5. *Applying Design Patterns:* Employ the use of design patterns like the Factory Pattern and Observer Pattern.

7.4. Mitigating Distant Changes

The other side of the coin is 'Distant Changes,' in situations where changes to a particular part involves modifications distributed across various unrelated parts of the system. It may sound contrasting, but it often goes hand in hand with 'Coupled Code.' As the code gets more coupled, changes get more widespread.

7.5. Identifying Distant Changes

Identifying distant changes can sometimes be trickier than spotting coupled code. If you're finding that a single feature change requires adjustments across multiple classes or modules, then congrats: you have stumbled upon distant changes.

7.6. Strategies for Managing Distant Changes

To manage distant changes, here are some strategies you can use:

1. *Demeter's Law:* This is a specific form of loose coupling. It restricts the number of objects you interact with and also the way you come to interact with them.

2. *Data Hiding:* Do not expose the internal data representation of an object beyond its boundaries.

3. *Encapsulate the Concept that Changes:* Encapsulate the part that changes or varies, separating the behavior that varies from the behavior that stays the same.

4. *Use Observer Pattern:* Whenever a subject undergoes changes, all dependents on the object would be notified about the change.

5. *Refactor Iteratively:* Over time, iteratively refactor your code to improve encapsulation, remove code redundancy, and better organize your program.

7.7. Conclusion

Refactoring to delete code smells is an ongoing proactive activity, requiring the correct diagnosis of the problem and the application of the appropriate solution. Remember, good designs come from understanding relationships between classes and other program elements, an essential perspective to have during the process of removing unnecessary dependencies. However, ensure tests exist before embarking any refactoring journeys; tests are the lifesavers that ensure refactoring does not break existing functionalities. Happy Refactoring!

Chapter 8. Complex Conditionals and Function Overloads: Simplifying the Complicated

It's a matter of common occurrence that a seemingly innocent piece of code can metamorphose into an intricate mass over time, embodying a variety of conditions and function overloads. The protagonist of our narrative here revolves around complex conditionals and function overloads, two phenomena regularly whipped in the annals of 'code smells'. Let's dissect these phenomena, perceive their mal-effects, and most importantly, learn the art of simplifying what appears complicated.

8.1. Understanding Complexity in Conditions and Overloads

When we talk about complexity in conditionals, it is the branching logic based on specific conditions, often nested or chained. Complex conditionals tend to reduce code readability, make testing difficult, and are a breeding ground for bugs.

Similarly, function overloads can sometimes lead to a bloated codebase, moreover causing confusion with multiple functions with the same name but different parameters. This could even result in unintended or unpredictable program behaviour if not carefully managed.

Unraveling the complexity of these elements is akin to untangling a knotted string: it requires effort, patience, but also proven techniques - the subject of our in-depth exploration in subsequent sections.

8.2. Reducing Conditional Complexity

Let's first tackle the beast of complex conditionals. A few strategies to mitigate this problem are:

1. Breaking down complex conditionals into simpler parts

2. Employing meaningful boolean methods

3. Deploying polymorphism where possible

Starting with the first, large conditionals could often be decomposed into smaller, simpler units. That way, you make the code more understandable and easy to maintain.

```
[.source]
```

```
if (temperature >= 30 && humidity > 50) { console.log('Hot and humid weather'); } else if (temperature < 5 && windSpeed > 20) { console.log('Cold and windy weather'); }

const isHotAndHumid = () => temperature >= 30 && humidity > 50;
const isColdAndWindy = () => temperature < 5 && windSpeed > 20;

if (isHotAndHumid()) { console.log('Hot and humid weather'); } else if (isColdAndWindy()) { console.log('Cold and windy weather'); }
```

Breaking conditionals clearly improves the readability and maintainability of the code.

Next, we could replace complex conditionals with boolean methods — offering outstanding legibility benefits.

Finally, polymorphism, a core concept in Object-Oriented

Programming (OOP), allows us to replace conditional logic with structured and reusable code blocks. This approach considerably simplifies the code and makes it more flexible and robust.

=== Function Overloads: Identifying and Simplifying

Insignificant in isolation, function overloads can contribute to code mess when overused or improperly managed. A few ways to simplify overloaded functions include using default arguments, employing optional methods, and leveraging generics.

Default arguments mitigate the need for an overload by providing standard values. If the function is called without certain parameters, the default parameters step in.

Optional parameters operate similar to defaults, but with slight variation. In languages like TypeScript, we could make a parameter optional by adding a '?' after the parameter name, eliminating the need of overloaded functions for multiple signatures.

Generics also play an essential role in reducing the need for function overloads. For statically typed languages like Java or C++, you can use generics to create functions that can work with different types of data.

These techniques, when appropriately used, can drastically reduce the convolution arising due to function overloads, making your code more readable, scalable and simple.

=== A Pragmatic Approach to Refactoring

Simply understanding 'what' to refactor doesn't suffice;
we must also grasp 'how' to refactor. The solution ▯ a
three-step approach:

. Identify the code smell
. Prioritize refactoring
. Implement the code changes

Identification forms the bedrock. Get to know your code
intimately. Look for potential reasons causing the
complexity. There's no 'one size fits all' solution, and
each case underpins a custom approach.

Prioritization is integral to successful refactoring.
Not all code smells can be addressed simultaneously.
Prioritize based on the degree of complexity, the impact
potential, and the time you're willing to devote to the
debugging process.

Finally, implementation. This is where you begin to
apply the techniques mentioned earlier. Remember, the
key to refactoring isn't making huge, sweeping changes
all at once, but changing the code incrementally,
verifying at each step if you're moving towards a
cleaner, simpler and better-quality codebase.

=== In Conclusion

Complex conditionals and function overloads can
trivialize the task of understanding, maintaining and
expanding a codebase. Hence, elevating your
understanding of these concepts and acquiring
proficiency in mitigating their adverse impacts can
considerably enhance your programming performance.

The journey towards mastering the art of simplifying
complex code necessitates diligence and patience.
Remember, each refactoring exercise, whether big or
small, tequilas incremental enhancements that aggregate
into a significant improvement over time.

Embark on this journey with an open mind, eager to
learn, and ready to make mistakes. After all, every
mistake is a learning opportunity, just a refactor away
from perfection.

== Practical Steps to Refactor: Taking the First Leap
In your programming journey, code refactoring becomes an
inevitable part of the software development lifecycle.
It's the process of fine-tuning the internal structure
of an existing body of code, without altering its
external behavior. Before diving into the practical
steps, it is prudent to remember the Golden Rule of
refactoring: always ensure that your code works before
you start refactoring, at all points during the process,
and after refactoring.

=== Recognizing Code Smells

Your first step is recognizing 'code smells.' Code
smells are symptoms in the code that indicate deeper
problems. They don't stop the program from functioning,
but significantly hamper its expansibility,
comprehensibility, and maintenance. Some common smells
are duplicated code, large functions, long parameter
lists, and feature envy. Recognizing these smells is a
skill that gains refinement with time and experience.

=== Ensuring Test Coverage

Now that you understand code smells, the next step

towards refactoring relies heavily on unit tests. Unit
tests are crucial because they provide a safety net,
allowing you to refactor with confidence. If your code
is not already under test, write tests before you
refactor. Ensure that tests adequately cover all the
main code pathways.

=== Formulate a Plan

Refactoring should be performed systematically, rather
than in a haphazard manner. It is vital that you not
bite off more than you can chew by trying to refactor
all at once. Instead, start with a small chunk of code
or a single 'smell.' Map out what transformations are
needed, and where you need to make these changes.
Prioritize the areas that are most urgent or will
provide the most immediate benefits.

=== Refactoring in Tiny Steps

Refactoring should never be done in huge chunks. Always
approach it incrementally. As Martin Fowler in his
seminal book on refactoring advises, "Refactor in small
steps...make a change, run the tests, make another
change, run the tests, repeat." Each individual step may
seem trivial, but the cumulative effect really enhances
the code without ever disrupting its functionality.

=== Using Tool Support

To implement the planned transformations, you will need
some tools. Modern Integrated Development Environments
(IDEs) incorporate many automated refactoring tools,
which can conduct a series of small transformations
efficiently while checking the impact on the overall
system. Don't be afraid to leverage these tools; they

are designed to make your work easier and more
effective.

=== Continuous Review and Refactoring

Remember that refactoring is not a one-time activity but
an ongoing process. There's always room to improve even
after your first attempt at refactoring. So, keep
improving your codebase by undertaking the refactoring
process from time to time. Don't let your code stagnate.
Be ready to review and refactor as needed.

=== Documenting the Refactoring

Documentation is a significant part of refactoring.
Other developers must understand why specific changes
were made, what impacted the decisions, and how to
extend or maintain this code in the future. This aspect
is especially critical if many developers are working on
the project or if the project may be developed further
in the future.

For each of these steps, remember that the primary aim
of refactoring is to simplify the design of existing
code, making it easier for you and others to understand
and modify. By carefully breaking down these steps and
working through them systematically, you can improve
your code without worrying about introducing bugs.
Remember that refactoring is an investment — a little
time spent here can save vast amounts of time in the
future. Dive in, and embrace the adventure of
refactoring!

== Tools and Techniques to Aid Refactoring
Refactoring involves restructuring an existing body of
code, changing the factoring without changing its

external behavior. The aim is to improve the design of existing code, making it more readable, maintainable, and extensible while preserving its functionality. This process can be challenging without appropriate tools and techniques to aid programmers. It is vital to equip ourselves with robust and effective software, methods, and best practices that can help in carrying out code refactoring efficiently and effectively. Let's delve into these tools and techniques.

=== Developer's Mindset

The first, and perhaps the most crucial tool in your refactoring arsenal, is your mindset. Refactoring isn't about changing what the code does. It's about changing how it does it. Embrace the mindset of continuous improvement. The journey towards better code isn't a destination ▯ it's a process. Each time you engage with your code, you should aspire to leave it better than you found it. Utilising a problem-solving mindset to critically assess the state of your code is the key to successful refactoring.

=== Automated Refactoring Tools

Different integrated development environments (IDEs) provide automated tools to refactor your code. These tools can detect bad code smells and suggest potential refactoring solutions, helping to automate and streamline the refactoring process.

IntelliJ IDEA, for instance, offers a list of automated refactoring options such as changing signatures, extracting variables or methods, inline variable or method, moving methods or variables, and more. Similarly, Eclipse IDE provides automated refactoring under the ⸢Refactor⸥ tab.

Using such automated refactoring tools is recommended as
it helps in reducing manual effort and the possibility
of human error. But exercise caution, as blindly
following these suggestions may introduce bugs or alter
code behavior. It's always critical to understand these
suggestions before implementation, reinforcing the fact
that automated tools should complement, not replace,
human judgment and skill.

=== Testing Frameworks

Comprehensive tests are essential during refactoring to
ensure that the behavior of the code remains consistent
even after the code changes. Unit tests work best for
this purpose and represent the minimum level of testing
that should be performed while refactoring.

Testing frameworks such as JUnit (for Java), PyTest (for
Python), RSpec (for Ruby), NUnit (.NET), Jest (for
JavaScript) provide features for asserting the output of
the code, A/B testing, mocking, and more.

Having tests written before refactoring helps catch any
unintended changes to functionality or behavior,
ensuring that your refactoring process doesn't break
existing code. This approach is known as Test-Driven
Development (TDD).

=== Version Control Systems

Version control systems are vital tools that help you
track changeRes to your source code, making it easier to
revert changes if a refactoring exercise results in bugs
or breaks your application. Git, SVN, Mercurial are a

few examples of version control systems. All changes, including refactors, should be committed and documented in version control systems to maintain a record of code evolution, facilitating better collaboration and bug tracking.

=== Code Review

Refactoring should also involve regular code reviews to ensure that the changes you make improve the code quality and don't introduce new bad smells or bugs. Regular code reviews with peers or senior developers can give you new perspectives on your code and point out potential issues or improvements you may have overlooked.

Online tools like GitHub, Bitbucket, or GitLab offer code review functionality, where you can open pull requests or merge requests to get your code changes reviewed by others before they are merged into the main codebase.

=== Design Patterns

Once you have detected bad smells and planned for refactoring, understanding design patterns can help you decide how to refactor the code effectively. Design patterns are time-tested solutions to common software design problems. They can be structural, creational, or behavioral, and guide you on how to structure your classes and objects to solve certain problems.

=== Linters and Static Code Analyzers

Linters and static code analyzers like ESLint (JavaScript), Pylint (Python), Checkstyle (Java) can

help you identify potential problems—like code smells,
bugs, style issues, and more— in your codebase without
running it. These tools play a crucial role in
maintaining the health of your codebase and making the
refactoring process more manageable and efficient.

Let's summarize what we've covered so far: Embrace a
developer's mindset of continuous improvement, utilize
automated refactoring tools but with caution, engage
comprehensive testing frameworks, version control
systems for tracking changes, regular code reviews for
maintaining code quality, design patterns for effective
refactoring, and linters and static code analyzers for
identifying potential issues.

However, keep in mind, tools are only as effective as
the wielder. In addition to utilizing these resources,
it is critical to understanding the underlying tenets of
clean code, and being conscientious about applying them
in every aspect of programming. As you continue on your
journey of developing code excellence, remember that
consistent practice and unending curiosity are the
ultimate keys to mastery.

== Maintaining Code Health: Best Practices for Ongoing
Code Quality
In the relentless pursuit of delivering top-notch
software applications, maintaining the health of your
code is as tantamount as writing it. This encompasses
robust use of techniques and paradigms to constantly
refactor and improve the codebase. This might feel
cumbersome and unnecessary, but the importance of
maintaining code health cannot be overstressed as it
directly impacts the productivity of the team,
scalability of the software and overall software
execution performance.

=== The Importance of Code Health

The vitality of code health is pivotal in the realm of
software development. Good health of code reduces the
time spent on bug fixing and allows easier feature
implementation. An unambiguous and well-managed codebase
promotes better understanding of the system across the
team. New team members can ramp up more quickly, and
efficient cross-team collaborations can be achieved. In
the long run, maintaining code health is economical as
it reduces the cost associated with system enhancements
and changes.

=== Aspects of Code Health

Code health encompasses several aspects:

1. *Readability*: Well-documented code is effortlessly
understandable and easy to maintain. In simple terms,
the code should reveal its intentions and necessities
without additional explanations or discussions. Always
remember, we write code for humans not machines.
2. *Modularity and encapsulation*: Keeping your code
modular promotes separation of concerns. This will lead
to better testing, improved cohesion, and reduced
coupling. It also ensures that the functionality of one
module is not affected by changes in another.
3. *Consistency*: Adopting a consistent coding style can
make the entire codebase easier to understand for
everyone involved. An inconsistent coding structure
often leads to unnecessarily complex, unreadable codes.
4. *Testability*: The degree to which your code can be
tested often mirrors its quality. Well-planned unit
tests, integration tests, and end-to-end tests ensure
all pieces of your code work in harmony.

5. *Performance*: Optimized code minimizes resource
wastage, ensuring high performance. It focuses on
reducing algorithmic complexity and unnecessary memory
consumption.

=== Ensuring Code Health: Best Practices

The first step towards maintaining code health is
understanding the best practices:

1. *Peer code review*: This practice promotes collective
code ownership while mitigating the risk of single-point
failures. Code reviews ensure that multiple eyes have
inspected the solution for its correctness, readability,
and alignment with the overall system's architecture.
2. *Regular refactoring*: Keeping the code clean should
be an ongoing process. Regular refactoring not only
increases the readability of the code, but it also
ensures that the design of the system evolves with its
needs.
3. *Writing tests*: Write unit, integration, and end-to-
end tests to ensure your code is working as intended. It
makes the code robust by ensuring functionality does not
break with newly added features or changes in existing
ones.
4. *Continuous Integration and Continuous Deployment
(CI/CD)*: This practice ensures that the code is
compiled, tested, and ready for release at all times. It
mitigates the risks associated with integration and
deployment and allows us to find and fix issues faster.
5. *Code metrics*: Evaluation of various code metrics
like cyclomatic complexity, duplication, code churn can
provide quantifiable data on the code health. These
should be regularly measured, monitored and improved.

=== Strategies for Implementing Code Health Practices

At this stage, understanding how to put these practices into play becomes crucial.

1. Schedule time for refactoring: It might seem counterproductive, but taking the time to organize and refine your code can save substantial effort, reduce bugs, and result in more stable software. Set aside some time within each sprint for refactoring tasks.

2. Enforce peer code review process: Make code review a necessary step before merging. Peer reviewing can shed light on potential issues that might have been overlooked, and it fosters a culture of collective code ownership.

3. Automate testing: Automate whenever possible. Automated testing greatly reduces the possibility of human error and improves code coverage. This will save time for areas that need manual testing.

4. Leverage tools : There are various static code analysis tools, code review tools, build automation tools available to aid in maintaining code health. Tools can help reduce manual effort and enforce quality check for every commit that goes in the repository.

5. Training and knowledge sharing: Understanding the deeper considerations of each practice, like functional programming, object-oriented design, domain-driven design, SOLID principles, etc., will empower the development team to write effective and high-quality code. Regular training sessions and knowledge sharing meetings serve as a great platform to ensure the whole team is on the same page and aware of good practices.

In conclusion, maintaining code health is an art that every development team should master. A positive code health check guarantees that the software system can evolve with changing requirements over time without significant degradation in its performance or maintainability.